Love Letters

for the

Romantically Challenged!

Rhonda R. Holmes

The Impact of Love Letters

I sold love letters individually printed on parchment paper with a matching envelope on a very small scale before finally putting them together in a book which from the beginning, customers had suggested I do—but I never saw them as something anyone would want to read in a book. I also felt it was not my business to ask questions about the recipient's response, because the love letters are personal. However, there were some customers who saw me after the love letter had been given to a lover/friend and thanked me without me having asked anything. I was grateful that someone was actually paying me for words that I had written.

* Deidre bought the love letter entitled, "I Love You, because…." and mailed it to her husband. "He never told me he received it. As I was putting his clothes away, I found it hidden underneath his underwear in the dresser drawer. I asked him about it and he told me, he liked it very much. He usually just put cards aside, but this time, he tucked the love letter away for safe keeping.

* Joseph was going through changes in his relationship. He bought, "How Can You Doubt My Love." There was a sentence in the third verse that he was uncomfortable with and asked if it could be changed. I don't make changes. However, when I saw him the next day, he paid for the love letter and thanked me.

* Jennifer bought "My Sensuous Lover" for her gentleman friend. She begged me to customize it with their names and offered to pay extra. I delivered the love letter to her on Friday. She liked the presentation, said it was pretty. I charged $10.00 for the love letter and she paid $10.00 extra for adding the names. She called me the following Monday to thank me. Her gentleman friend had been flabbergasted and told her no one had ever given him anything like that. He personally came to her job that morning to bring her a dozen roses.

* Ken bought love letters every few months from the "Friendship" category. At one point, he bought four love letters at one time and later said they were a hit.

* Larry, referred by Ken also bought love letters every few months from the "Friendship" category. At one point, he bought two love letters for a new girlfriend and mailed them. After receiving them, the girlfriend called him, read the love letters aloud and cried. She said they were so touching, and if he had signed them, it would have been perfect.

* Paula was from Columbia, interning in NYC at the UN. She sent her boyfriend the love letter, "I Miss You," by her brother who was returning home after vacationing in New York. He wanted to buy a love letter for his girlfriend, but there wasn't time to choose one. After receiving the love letter, Paula's boyfriend taped the love letter to the inside of his bedroom closet door so that each time he opened it, he thought of her.

* 'Michael' bought "You Intoxicate My Soul." The next day, he gave me the thumbs up and stated that the person who received it told him it was perfect and the love letter said just the right thing.

* 'Josephine,' who did not confide in me about the response she received from "The Seduction Fantasy," purchased it on two separate occasions.

* One customer called from Florida to say that he found a brochure of mine in his closet after four years. He was proposing to his girlfriend on her birthday. He bought four love letters that I helped him choose over the phone and sent to him by mail.

One-of-kind Custom Poems
Given as Anniversary/Wedding Gifts

* Nancy requested something special for a couple she knew celebrating their 40th wedding anniversary. She wanted something unique and different. She gave me a few details about their relationship. She spoke to the couple's daughter about the poem she was having written and the daughter was excited! Nancy couldn't make the anniversary party, but she had the poem framed in glass with beveled edges. I was given a copy of the thank you card she received. It read, *Dearest Nancy, you really "out did" yourself with the most unique poem to us as we celebrate our fortieth wedding anniversary. The poet knew what to write. It is on the wall in our bedroom. We love it!* The anniversary poem was entitled *"Forty Years Together...and Our Love Continues to Grow."*

* Valerie wanted something for her sister's sixth wedding anniversary. The anniversary poem is entitled, *"Our Love Has Only Just Begun."* I never knew what her sister's response to the gift was until I was visiting at the home that they shared. Without asking, her sister walked into the living room carrying a large matted picture frame. She showed it to me—as I had not seen it after I wrote it —and thanked me. I stated that I wrote it, but it was a gift from her sister. She said, I could have written something corny.

* I was invited to a wedding and did not have money for a gift. After the success of the first two anniversary poems, I decided to write one for myself as a gift to the couple. It was entitled, *"The Future is Ours."* I had it customized in a black and gold wood speckled frame. The poem itself was printed on gold parchment paper. Five months later, I received a thank you card. It read, *Dear Rhonda, Thank you for the wonderful poem. We have it displayed in our bedroom. It is a special gift and we love it so much. No one has been as creative or original as you.*

Personal Note

In writing these love letters, I wanted each one to be very special. I wanted to write in such a way as to elicit an emotional response--to touch a chord at the center of someone's heart. I wanted each person who reads one of these love letters to feel the passion in which they were written. I try to dig deep down into my soul to enable me to write from my heart which is often filled with emotion and sensuality. I want to express what is difficult for others to express either verbally or in writing--to a lover or friend.

In writing about love, you have to experience life in its joy and sorrow. You must be in touch with your feelings. You must be in touch with the issues that men and women deal with in their lives together. I wanted to write about what I thought someone might want to express to a lover or friend. Each relationship goes through different stages of development from friendship to possible marriage. Although, not all relationships begin with friendship and not all relationships develop into a lasting romance, I wanted to write love letters that were a reflection of these changes and stages in life.

TABLE OF CONTENTS

FRIENDSHIP (cont'd)

FEELINGS OF LOVE

FEELINGS OF LOVE (cont'd)

MISSING YOU

PROPOSAL

PROPOSAL (cont')

APOLOGY

END OF RELATIONSHIP

FANTASY OF LOVE

REFLECTION

REFLECTION (cont'd)

DESCRIPTION OF CATEGORIES

"Love Letters for the Romantically Challenged!" is for those men and women who don't have time to write something personal, passionate or intimate as well as for those whose writing skills may not be as sharp as they would like and for those who may have difficulty in expressing their thoughts. These love letters try to convey thoughts and feelings that many of us may experience in our relationships and may want to express either verbally or in print. The love letters are divided into eight themes:

* "*Friendship*"- Love letters for two people in a relationship, but who are not yet in love. However, at least one person in the relationship wishes to express sentiments that are emotional and personal. The word 'love' is never used in this category.

* "*Feelings of Love*" - Love letters for men and women who are in love and want to express those feelings. These love letters are for old and new loves and cover a variety of situations involving feelings of love.

* "*Missing You*" - Love letters for those who want to express how much they miss and want to be with their lover and/or friend.

* "*Proposal*" - Love letters for those who want to be with a lover in a long lasting permanent relationship. These love letters do not outright ask the lover for their hand in marriage, but suggests a future together.

* "*Apology*" - Love letters for men and women who need to apologize for an action or deed that they did or did not do.

* "*End of Relationship*" - Love letters for men and women who are ending their relationship; who may be on the verge of ending their relationship; or who may be trying to save their relationship.

* "*Fantasy of Love*" - Love letters for men and women with a fantasy that they want to share with their lover and/or friend.

* "*Reflection*" - is a category of thoughts that reflect the human experience from various perspectives.

Love is Universal

It touches everyone throughout their lives. Love is a part of life from birth until death. There are different stages and levels of love: love for oneself; between parent and child; between friends; between lovers and the greatest love of all, love for mankind. However, romantic love between two people can be one of the most fulfilling--emotionally, physically, and spiritually.

Three Stages of Love

LUST

1. Intense or unrestrained sexual craving.

INFATUATION

1. A foolish, unreasoning, or extravagant passion or attraction.

2. An object of extravagant, short lived passion.

LOVE

1. A deep, tender, ineffable feeling of affection and solicitude toward a person, such as that arising from kinship, recognition of attractive qualities, or a sense of underlying oneness.

(Definitions taken from the American Heritage Dictionary)

Friendship

A true love relationship sometimes
begins with a friendship, however a
friendship doesn't always lead to a
love relationship. Friendship in itself
is something to be treasured.

I Can't Get You Out of My Mind!

*I have been fantasizing about you since
the day we met, because you have
awakened in me, a hunger for intimacy,
I have not felt in some time.*

*I think about you everyday and long to
spend time with you just to talk about
life, love and the pursuit of happiness
while being lured by your presence.*

*So, I'm asking you at this moment, let's get
together this week. We can discuss what we
want to do and where we want to do it,
because I can't get you out of my mind!*

I Would Like to Go Out With You

I was wondering ... if you would honor me with your presence, because I would like to take you to breakfast, lunch or dinner and a movie, whichever is more convenient for you.

I'm attracted to you and would like to get to know you. You seem like the type of person who would appreciate the finer things in life and whose mind, I'd like to explore.

There are no strings attached. I would just like to spend time with you, and if the attraction is mutual, then we can take it from there.

Will you go out with me?

I Enjoy Spending Time with You

It's nice just to be able to sit and talk with you about what makes the world go round without having to pretend to be someone or something that I am not.

It is the simple pleasures in life that are most precious and knowing you has added to the quality of my existence.

So, I'd like to continue to get together, whether it's to go to dinner, see a movie, or talk about nothing in particular, because I enjoy spending time with you.

I Like You Very Much

*I like you very much and since
action speaks louder than
words, I'm going to sweep you
off your feet and steal your
heart away.*

*You're all I think about
morning, noon and night. I
think about being with you and
holding you tight.*

*I want thoughts of me to keep
you up all night. I want to be
the one you can't live without,
because I like you so very much.*

Whenever You Need a Friend, I'll be There

If you ever need someone to talk to, I will listen. If you ever need to cry, I will give you my shoulder. Even if you just need someone to keep you company, just call me.

Any time of the day or night, whenever you need a friend, I'll be there. Through rain, sleet or snow, I'll be there to hold you, comfort you and to heal you.

But I want you to call not only when you need to be consoled. I want you to call me when life is good and treating you well.

You Have Touched Me in Ways that You'll Never Know

I have never met anyone who has stirred up such deep feelings within me without having had any physical contact. Yet, you have done so, without even trying.

You have made me see things that I have never noticed before, and you have made me feel things that I have never known existed inside of me.

My life has been enhanced since I have met you. If I never feel this way again, I am privileged to have felt this way at least once in my lifetime. . . .

You Never Stop Caring

You probably don't realize the impact
you've had on my life. The things you do,
though small or simple are very
meaningful, although you may not think
of it as a big deal. But, it's the little
things in life that really matter. However,
that's just the type of person you are, you
do things from the heart.

Your arms are always open, whenever I
need someone to lean on . . . silently, or
whenever I need to let it all out. You
never criticize me even though I may be
deserving of it, sometimes. I appreciate
your time, your patience, your advice,
and I appreciate you.

I want you to know that you are a
special part of my life. I could never
forget the difference you have made in
the way I view the world. You will
always hold a special place in my heart.
So, I just want to tell you how much I
care for you, because you never stop
caring for me.

You Opened the Door to My Heart

You have no idea of the effect you have on me. You never ask for anything in return, but you are always giving of yourself and never turn me away whenever I turn to you for help.

You opened the door to my heart, because you take everything in stride and accept me as I am. There's no strain between us when silence rules, and when I need to be alone, you don't take it personally.

You don't pretend to like everything that I do, but you always tell me exactly how you feel. So, I never feel ashamed or embarrassed to express my feelings to you.

I'd Like to Take Our Friendship Further

I find myself thinking about you more often than not in a way I haven't considered before. I think we have a great friendship, and I don't want to destroy it in any way. But, I have to admit that I'm finding myself attracted to you. I don't want to make you uncomfortable, but I have to tell you how I feel.

We've always enjoyed each other's company and we can talk about anything, because that's what friends do for one another. We respect each other and what I like about you as a person, I like very much.

I'm ready to take our friendship further. If you decide that this is something you may want to pursue—you don't have to decide right away. I know you may need time to think about how you feel, and I'm fine with that. Whatever your decision, I'll accept it. I don't want it to change the nature of our relationship, if you don't feel the same way. If you do decide that you'd like to take our friendship further, I'm more than ready to go out on our first date.

I'd Like to be More
Than Just Friends

You know when I am happy and sense
when I am down. You know when to
comfort me without smothering me. We
have no secrets from each other, because
our love as friends is unconditional.

But, I want to be more than just friends.
I want to wine you and dine you and
treat you like royalty, not because I
want to make love to you, but because
that is how it should be.

I don't want to hurt our relationship. I
only want to add icing on the cake,
because loving you could only take our
relationship into a higher orbit, if you're
willing to reach for the stars.

Are you willing to take a chance?

I'm Ready to Make
a Commitment

I like you so very much, and I know how you feel about me. I enjoy listening to the sound of your voice, and I always look forward to seeing your face.

I love the way you make me feel like no one else ever has, and I share your ideas for the future. We want the same things out of life.

You wanted a commitment that I did not want to make. I was afraid of committing myself to someone who may not be as committed to me. So, if you still feel the same way, I'm ready to make a commitment to you, now.

*I Want You to Believe
and Trust in Me*

*I want you to know how much I
care about you and how much I
would like you to be a part of my
life.*

*I also know that some things take
time, and I don't want to force
you into anything. I do know
that you need to believe and to
trust in me.*

*So, I'm going to do what I need
to do to win you over, so that you
will have no doubt about
anything that I do or say. All I
want to do is be with you.*

Do You Want to be With Me?

I admire the qualities you possess and the way you carry yourself. You're what I want in a human being. I've enjoyed the time we've spent together, and I believe you've enjoyed it as well. I thought we had the beginnings of a relationship that I looked forward to nurturing.

I want to spend more time with you, getting to know more about you, understanding who and what you are inside. However, I get the sense that you don't want to be with me. You're avoiding me. If that is so, I would like to know why? I hope I haven't offended you in any way. I thought we were equally interested in each other.

Maybe you need time to figure out your own thoughts. I don't have a problem with giving you time, if that's what you feel you need, but please . . . tell me something! I need to know . . . do you want to be with me?

We Can Take it One Day at a Time

I want to get to know everything about you. I want you to learn all you can about me, because I feel something special can develop between us.

I'm willing to take it slow, if that's what you want to do, because all I want to do is spend more time with you and show you how much I care.

I want us to feel comfortable with each other in everything that we do or say. We can take it one day at a time, because you are worth every second, every minute and every hour. If we are meant to be together, then time has no limitations.

You're Worth Waiting For

*I will never stand in the way of your
pursuing your goals now or in the future.
Whatever length of time you feel you
need to accomplish your goals, I'll be
standing right by your side, if you let me.*

*I won't rush you into making any
decisions about our relationship.
I do, however, want to share in your
happiness and your success.*

*I also want you to know how loving,
understanding and patient I can
be, because anything worth having is
worth waiting for, and I'll be waiting
for you. . . .*

I Want You in My Life ... Always

*Although, we may not see each other
every day or talk on the phone, it
doesn't mean that I am not thinking
about you. I have thoughts of you
every day.*

*And each time, I do hear your voice,
I feel my day has been fulfilled, and
I am comforted by the knowledge
that I have you in my life.*

*So, when we do spend time together,
nothing else in life seems to matter,
but the memories that will last
forever, that's when I realized, I
want you in my life ... always.*

You are My Sweetheart . . .

*You are the object of my desires and
you make my world go round,
because you are important in my life.
I enjoy being with you, if only for a
second, a minute or an hour, because
you are my sweetheart. . . .*

*The time we spend together, whether
going out or staying in is time I'll
always remember, memories that will
last forever. You are my
sweetheart. . . .*

*I will try to minimize any pain and
prolong your happiness, because when
you hurt . . . I hurt. When you are
happy . . . I am happy. You are
my sweetheart. . . .*

You're Always on My Mind

It seems I can't stop thinking about you. I can't get you out of my mind. It doesn't matter how much time we spend together, because when we're apart, I'm thinking of you . . . always.

I can't breathe without thinking about you. I can't sleep without dreaming about the look in your eyes. All I want to do . . . is hold you in my arms tonight.

I want to be with you for all the reasons that a man wants a woman and a woman wants a man. I want to be with you, because you make me feel good inside, that's why you're always . . . on my mind.

All I Do is Think About You....

Time and time again, my thoughts are interrupted as I sit around contemplating the depth to which you have unconsciously unleashed feelings that I have consciously tried to keep at a distance.

I feel exhilarated and intimidated at the same time. Exhilaration comes from the excitement and energy careening throughout my body at just the sight of you. Intimidation, because of expectations, I may not be able to fulfill.

I want nothing more than to be with you in every way. I want to explore that part of you that has so eloquently forced me to expose myself emotionally. Furthermore . . . all I do is think about you. . . .

I Never Stopped
Thinking about You

Though time and distance has come between us, I never stopped thinking about you. What we shared is not forgotten, because history can never be erased.

I'd like to think our time together was meaningful in its own way. I'd like to believe that each phase of my life had an impact on the person I've become.

Memories have a way of escaping one's thoughts involuntarily. The time spent with you was memorable and often unforgettable. I never stopped thinking about you. . . .

I Want to Thank You

*It is not often that I meet someone
like you, someone who is caring and
giving. Someone who is willing to
share and exchange knowledge and
life experiences.*

*The knowledge I have gained from you
and the assistance I have received is
invaluable. I can't begin to tell you
how powerful that makes me feel.*

*So, I want to thank you for sharing
and teaching. I want you to know
how much I appreciate all the guidance
you have given me.*

I Value Your Friendship

I can discuss anything with you, and
I always feel free to ask your opinion or
advice. When I need someone to talk to,
I know I can always call on you.

A friendship like yours is priceless, and I
am honored to have you as a friend. You
never ask why and you never judge me,
although you may not agree with what
I do or say.

I want to always be friends and never
lose touch. Regardless of how close
or how far apart we live from each
other, I value your friendship and
want to keep it alive.

True Friendship is not One-Sided

I thought a friendship was a relationship between two people sharing an intimacy of pain, happiness, secrecy and the most important, the ability to listen, console and understand without judging.

I feel that our friendship falls short of these characteristics. I am sometimes hurt by your lack of concern, when I am expressing my deep felt emotions and need your understanding and attention.

However, I am always ready to lend you my support when you are in need of consolation and understanding. I would like our friendship to be one in which we acknowledge and are sensitive to each other's concerns.

I Just Want to be Friends

I don't want to be the type of person who leads you on, because that is not my intention. However, I think you are a very sweet person, fun to be with, and I do enjoy conversing with you, but I just want to be friends.

I hope you are not offended. You can never have enough good friends. Everyone is not worthy of being called a friend, but I would very much like to consider you one of mine.

So, if it's alright with you, and I hope that it is, I would like to continue as friends. As friends, if you ever need someone to talk to, you can call on me. I will try to do what I can to help you, even if it means just listening.

Feelings of Love

Falling in love is an experience that
sometimes happen in a subtle way or may
explode overnight. It can be both spiritually,
emotionally and physically satisfying, but
only when that love is reciprocated, can
it be called true love. . . .

I'll Wait Forever for Your Love

I see your teardrops when it rains and
feel your pain on cloudy days. The
stars reflect the sparkle in your eyes
and your smile is radiant as a sunrise.

I know that you are not in love
with me as I am in love with you, but
you will always have my shoulder to
cry on and my ear to bend.

I want you to be a part of my life
even if it is just a friendship, because
no matter where you are or who you
are with, I'll wait forever for
your love.

I Think I'm Falling in
Love With You

I think I'm falling in love with you,
and I don't know what to do. I
don't want to scare you away, but
wonder if what I feel is real.

Whether we're alone or in a crowd,
the only face I see belongs to you.
The only sound I hear comes from
your lips. Nothing else exists but
our own space and time.

I think of you day and night and
wonder how often do you think of
me? Now that I've exposed my heart
to you, where do we go from here?

I'm So in Love With You

There is no other way to say this than to say it. I am so in love with you. . . . I wasn't looking for love, but you happened upon me, anyway.

I realized, I was in love with you, when I began noticing things about you . . . things no one else would notice. I realized, I was in love with you, when I looked forward to sharing my thoughts with you. I realized, I was in love with you, when the ache in my heart surfaced even before you said, good night.

Feeling the way that I do, I can only say, I'm so in love with you. I wasn't looking for love, but you happened upon me . . . anyway.

I Can't Envision Living
My Life Without You

I wake up every morning, and I go
to sleep each night with the scent of
your being permeating the air that
I breathe.

You penetrate the depth of my soul
with your eyes and never fail to
intoxicate me with your kiss.

Your understanding of life is
profound, yet you are able to enjoy
the simple things it has to offer.

How could I not be smitten by you?

I Want to Make Love to You All Night

I'll sprinkle rose petals on white satin sheets, place a bottle of Perignon on the side, then meet you at the door in my birthday suit tied in red ribbon, wearing a smile.

But I can only love you, if you want to be loved. So, I'll seduce your mind and then your body and fulfill any fantasy you may have, because I want to make love to you all night.

After dessert, we'll have a late dinner while I savor the memories of our ecstasy, because every moment that we spend together, I want to remember forever and ever....

I Love You because. . .

I may not say it very often, but I do love you. I may not kiss you or hug you as much as I should, but I do love you. I may even have been wrong many times, but I do love you.

I love you, because you put up with me. I love you, because you ignore me when I shouldn't be taken seriously, but you ignore me in a nice way. I love you, because you are as beautiful on the inside as you are on the outside.

My love for you is never ending. You laughed with me through the good times and cried with me through the bad times, but we stuck together through it all. I can't think of anyone else, I would rather share my experiences with than you.

I love you because. . . you turn me on in every way!

No One Could Ever Love You
the Way That I Love You!

You came into my life at a time when I was at a crossroads. You gave me the space to discover what I wanted and needed in my life.

You became a friend that I could talk to whenever I needed someone to listen. I could always count on you to be there for me any time of the day or night.

So, I always expected you to be a part of my life. I took it for granted that you knew how I felt about you, because no one could ever love you the way that I love you. . . .

I Will Always Love You....

You are sensitive, compassionate and understanding. You never try to change who I am, but you seem to accept and acknowledge that we have our differences.

Your acceptance of my imperfections has made me vulnerable to you. So, when I look deep into your eyes, I see mirrors to your soul . . . and I am hypnotized by your loveliness.

You have brought meaning into my life, so I could never deny the love that I feel for you. I will always love you . . . till the end of time, because my love for you flows endlessly like a waterfall.

You're Everything I Have
Ever Wanted and More

Before you came into my life, I've had disappointments and heartbreaks. I never received the love I wanted, and the love I gave was never appreciated. So, I almost gave up on finding true love until we found each other.

You love me like I have never been loved before. When you kiss me, I always hunger for more. My body aches for hours long after your caress, but I know we'll love again and our love will never end.

You make me feel loved and needed, and I never feel ashamed to discuss what I'm feeling. We want the same things from life, and we know how to get it. I believe our love was meant to be, and I want you to know, you are everything I have ever wanted and more.

*Now That the Rough Times are Over,
I Need You to Spend Time with Me*

*When we joined together, it was for life
through good times and bad times. Sharing our
lives together means commitment, compromise
and sometimes sacrifice. Sometimes we sacrifice
the amount of time we spend together to allow
one or both of us to maintain our household
when times are rough.*

*But the rough times have passed and yet, we are
still spending time away from each other either
physically, emotionally or both. I want you in
my life forever, but I also need your love and
companionship, otherwise we'll grow apart
instead of growing together. You are the only
love in my life, and I love you like I have never
loved anyone else. So, you have no reason to
doubt my love, my faithfulness and my devotion.*

*I need you to hold me, to kiss me tenderly, and to
caress me long into the night like I am the only
one in the world for you. I need you to whisper
sweet nothings in my ear and shower me with
the attention that I deserve, because your love is
the only love that makes my heart flutter.*

I Don't Want to Hide
Our Love Anymore

*I admit that when we met, we
agreed to keep our relationship
hidden, because we didn't want to
hurt anyone. I can no longer abide
by those rules.*

*I can't go on pretending to be happy
about keeping our love affair secret.
I have fallen in love with you, and
I want to tell the world!*

*I don't mean to pressure you at
this time. I want you to make
a choice, and I hope that it is
me that you choose to love,
eternally. . . .*

You've Got to Take
Another Chance on Love!

I know that you have been hurt in the past by someone with whom you were in love. But, you cannot live in the past forever, because if you do, you deny me the opportunity to prove myself to you.

I can tell that you enjoy being with me, but you are afraid to become emotionally involved or to let your true feelings emerge. I can feel you holding back a precious part of yourself.

I would never hurt you. I want to get to know everything about you. We can take it one day at a time, but you've got to take another chance on love, because what I feel for you is very real.

I Need a Little Time

Although I have feelings for you, I am
not yet ready to take our relationship
further only because I want to be sure
that what we have is genuine and that
it is not just a fleeting moment in
time. . . .

When I give you my love, I give you
my body, my heart, and my soul. So, if
you really care for me, you'll take things
slowly, because I need a little time
before I surrender my love to you.

I believe my love is worth waiting for
and if we are destined to be together,
then nothing will keep us apart. I want
you to know, however, that my love is
relinquished only when my heart has
been filled.

Are You Afraid of Loving Me?

I don't know how much more I can express to you, verbally, physically or emotionally, the way I feel about you and how you make me feel. I have opened up my heart and exposed my inner self to you in ways I have never done with anyone else.

I want to love you in ways I have never believed I could love before. Do you know that I love everything about you? I love the small insignificant things that no one else would care about. I love the imperfections that make you unique as a person. Most of all, I love you. . . .

With all that I feel about you, I can't help but notice that you're not completely comfortable with sharing your feelings. You seem to be holding your feelings at bay. I want you to feel free to express how you feel about me.

Are you afraid of loving me?

How Can You Doubt My Love?

How can you doubt my love when all the love I have is for you? No one else puts a smile on my face, makes my heart skip a beat or send shivers up my spine each time our eyes meet.

I think of you every moment of every day and look forward to spending as much time with you as I can. When I am in your embrace or just sharing the same space, that's all I need to feel completely at ease.

Each time you place your hand upon my body, inside of me burns like flowing lava. Each kiss placed upon my lips leaves me feeling dazed and often breathless. So, how can you doubt my love, when the only one I love is you?

Our Love is Real . . .

*The power of your love is so
penetrating that just a fleeting glance
into your eyes sends a shiver of desire
racing throughout my body.*

*I feel so irresistibly sensual in your
presence that each time I walk out
the door, I must consciously remind
myself that this is real, that you are
real . . . our love is real. . . .*

*I love you so much. I can think
of nothing else, but tasting the sweet,
tender, longing of your lips against
mine each time our bodies embrace.*

How do I Choose, between the Two of You?

What I have to tell you is not easy to confess, because how do I tell you without hurting you that I am in love with you as well as someone else?

How do I tell you that I'm torn between loving you and another person and find it difficult to choose between you, because you are both very special in my life?

I didn't plan to fall in love with two people. I don't know how to handle my feelings, but I knew I had to be honest with you and with myself.

I Have Been in Love with You,
Secretly, for Some Time. . . .

For too long, I've held my feelings
hostage, fearing that any disclosure
of my deeply hidden love for you
would cause pain and destruction to
those around us.

It has been difficult living a lie,
pretending to be happy while inside,
my heart aches and my body hungers
for your touch. My only relief has been
in fantasizing about what could be. . . .

But now, with the passage of time and
a change in circumstances, I feel free to
share with you how I really feel . . . to
expose my heart and soul to tell you, I
have been in love with you, secretly,
for some time. . . .

I'd Like to be More Than Just Friends

You know when I am happy and sense when I am down. You know when to comfort me without smothering me. We have no secrets from each other because our love as friends is unconditional.

But, I want to be more than just friends. I want to wine you and dine you and treat you like royalty not because I want to make love to you, but because that is how it should be.

I don't want to hurt our relationship. I only want to add icing on the cake, because loving you could only take our relationship into a higher orbit, if you're willing to reach for the stars.

Are you willing to take a chance?

I Just Want to Love You

From the moment you seep into my consciousness, I often find myself breathless. As my eyes focus upon your face, I find it difficult to look away.

When you speak to me, my heart skips a beat, because the sound of your voice leaves me yearning for your touch.

I just want to love you and hold you close. I want to give you what no one else ever has, a part of my soul and a love that will last. . . .

All the Love I Feel is for You

I didn't plan to fall in love, so when
I fell in love with you, I didn't know
if what I felt was real or if I should
reveal to you how I feel.

But, I can't hide what I'm feeling
inside, because every thought,
every want and every need leaves my
hunger for you unfulfilled.

I want to wrap you in my arms and
kiss your tender lips. I want each
moment with you to last forever,
because all the love I feel is for you
and no other.

You're My One and Only Love

In the day, evening or night,
you're constantly on my mind. I
don't know what I'd do without
you, a love like yours is hard to
find.

I'm your friend and your lover.
Whatever your wants and desires,
all you have to do is ask, and I'll
do my best to light your fire.

You're my one and only love.
And, I want you to know that
my heart belongs to you, and
I'll never let you go.

I Just Want You to Know. . . .

*I just want you to know how much
I love you, baby. I want you by my
side, and I need you in my life.*

*I want to shower you with love
and affection. I'm willing to give
you all that I've got. All I want to
do is make you happy, because
loving you is what I do best.*

*I just want you to know, wherever
I go thoughts of you follow. I'll try
not to ever let you down, because I
want you to always be around.*

You Always Make Me Feel Wanted

When you hold me in your arms, I never want you to let go, because of the way you make me feel. You always make me feel wanted.

Sometimes, all I need is just to hear the sound of your voice, if only for a minute. Since you've become a part of my life, I'm never lonely.

I find myself constantly thinking of you and wanting you. But, most of all just knowing that you belong to me keeps me smiling inside, endlessly.

Jealousy Has No Place in Your Heart!

*I tell you constantly that my heart beats
only for you. I show you how much I
care, and I tell you how I feel, but you
still feel threatened if I just glance in
another direction.*

*If you do not believe in my love, how can
our relationship continue to grow? I feel
that I am always having to prove my
faithfulness and it is emotionally
draining for both of us. The energy could
be spent enhancing our love instead of
slowly and subtly pulling it apart.*

.

*As long as we are together, I will love
you the way that you want to be loved.
I will hold you when you need to be held
and give you all of me that I can give.
There should be no question in your mind
as to where my loyalties and heart lie.*

Loving You and Our New Baby

When you came into my life, I knew
you were the one for me. Each time
we met, I fell more in love with you.
All you had to do was smile and you
had me in the palm of your hand.

I couldn't go on without asking you to
be my forever love. We've been happy
ever since, and I didn't think our lives
could be any happier until you told me
we were having our first baby.

Now my life is complete. I can't ask
for anything more. I will love you till
the end . . . and our new baby too.
Loving you and our new baby is
what makes my life worthwhile.

My Sensuous Lover

To my darling with whom I am so deeply in love, you drive me wild with your endless passion so that each time we are together, you leave me completely drained and my energy level depleted.

What am I to do with you? I want so desperately to be with you every minute. . . . Yet, I think that it is better that I stay away just to re-energize my state of mind and body, lest you cripple me unintentionally.

However, it is difficult to keep you away from my thoughts. When we follow our own separate paths, visions of you appear wherever I go, because you have become a part of my subconscious.

You Intoxicate My Soul. . . .

Your body is an aphrodisiac. Each time, I place my hand upon it, heat flows slowly like burning embers from the tips of my fingers throughout the length of my body as I caress you tenderly long into the night.

Any thoughts I have other than you suddenly vanish and my mind becomes spellbound! Your lips sweet as honey, stimulating as wine leaves me feeling breathless with each kiss.

My whole being is rendered helpless in your presence as I become a slave to your love. My speech often becomes unintelligible. . . . And each time my fire is lit, I succumb more and more to your desires, because you intoxicate my soul. . . .

Our Love is So Sensuous

From the very moment that I sense your
lips touching and ever so gently caressing
the tender flesh of my body, a surge of
electricity flowing slowly throughout
creates an explosion of heat at the very
core of my being.

Our love is so sensuous that when we
are making love it is reminiscent of
an out of body experience that has me
soaring to great heights into an
unknown galaxy.

Oh darling, I don't know what I
would do without you in my life. You
always make me feel wanted when I need
to be loved and needed when I want to
belong.   We have the kind of love that
transcends time and space and our love is
so sensuous, because we are so deeply in
love. . . .

You're My Forever Love

I have never experienced a love such as yours, a love so physical and emotional, a love so deep and spiritual. Your love is all I have left to sustain me when I have nothing left at all.

I cannot imagine what my life would have been like had I never met you. Perhaps our paths were destined to meet as surely as the sun rises and sets each day.

You're my forever love. You're my only love. What we have together, no one can ever take apart, because our love for each other is strong and everlasting. . . .

I Love You . . . My Darling

*How can I express to you the many
ways in which I love you. . . . It is
difficult to express in words, the
fluttering of my heart at just the hint
of your presence.*

*My feelings for you are to such an
extreme that even I am afraid to
acknowledge or admit the meaning of
such depth. I cannot begin to
understand the emotional tenderness
I feel towards you. All I know is,
I love you . . . my darling. . . .*

*Perhaps, it is not to discover why I feel
this way, but to continue loving you
each and every way to stimulate your
mind and to satisfy your body.*

I'm Still in Love with You

I'm still in love with you, and I don't know
if that will ever change. How could I ever
fall out of love with you? Loving you has
strengthened my character, exposed my heart
and uncovered my emotions.

Loving you has left me feeling vulnerable at
times, and I often ask myself what has come
over me? The love I feel for you will never
fade away, entirely. It will linger on
forever . . . silently.

Love is such a complex and powerful
emotion, and I can't explain why I feel the
way that I do. All I know is that . . . I'm
still in love with you.

I Want Your Compassion
& Understanding

Baby, I know that I have not been
loving you the way that you are used
to being loved by me. You have to
understand that what I have just
been through was very difficult.

I love you with all my heart, but
I don't want to be loved by you,
right now. What I want from you is
your compassion and understanding
of what I have just gone through.

What I really need is for you to just
hold me in your arms and tell me that
you love me and that you'll wait
until I am ready to show my love for
you and to be loved by you again.

I Thought I'd Lost You

I never realized how much I really love you,
until I thought that I 'd lost you, and I'd
never see you again. You can't imagine the
emptiness and solitude that overcame me
and left me with an overwhelming sense of
dread and despair. A feeling so devastatingly
lonely. . . .

The disagreements and arguments we've had
seem so insignificant now. All that really
matters is that we have each other, still. If I
wasn't before, I am now more appreciative
of the little things that we do together and
the time that we share.

I'm more aware of your presence even when
you are not physically present. I hear your
voice even though you have not spoken, and
my skin tingles long after your touch.
Loving you and being with you has never
meant so much to me.

You Have Always Stood
by My Side

I am in love with you and that will
never change. Even though we have
disagreements, you respect my feelings
and never belittle my opinions, and you
always stand by the choices I make.

I may have done things in the past that
I am not proud of, but I have learned
from my mistakes. Life is a learning
experience, and you have taught me the
meaning of true love.

I want you to know how much you have
enriched my life. You are the best thing
that has ever happened to me. I can't
imagine loving anyone else but you. I
will love you forever. . . .

Loving You has Turned
My Life Around

*I didn't always have a sense of direction of
where my life was headed, nor did I necessarily
care. I probably took things for granted and
didn't feel the need to plan ahead or focus on
anything that might enhance my life in any
significant way.*

*But then . . . I met you. . . . I'm still not quite
sure what you did or how you did it, but I fell
in love with you. I find myself wanting to
make a difference in both our lives. I don't
take everything for granted anymore and your
happiness is a reflection of how much I can
contribute to making our lives satisfying
and fulfilling.*

*Loving you has turned my life around. You
gave me a sense of myself, I didn't know I was
lacking. I may not have been easy to deal with,
but you chose to be with me. All I can say
is . . . thank you for loving me.*

Sharing My Life with You is All I Ever Wanted

There comes a time in your life when you reflect back and remember your thoughts, your dreams, your desires, your goals and whether or not you have actually pursued those things that you felt at the time would be life affirming.

In my reflection, I've concluded that while I may not have accomplished each and every thing that was on my list, I am happy, because sharing my life with you is all I ever wanted. All the other things I may not have accomplished so far will be all the more exciting to pursue, because I can share the experiences with you.

There's nothing more freeing than being in your presence and feeling vulnerable, yet secure enough to expose you to my strengths as well as weaknesses, because I know that you will not take advantage of me when I am at my lowest point. I can't imagine not having you in my life.

I'll Do Anything for You

There's nothing I wouldn't do for you,
because your love has driven me to a
height of ecstasy that knows no bounds,
and when I am with you, you make me
believe that I can do anything.

Loving you has distracted me so, that I
forgive those whom I never would have
forgiven. I see beauty in those things that
others have condemned, and I am so
attuned to you that I sense your presence
long before you appear.

Our life together is a symphony of love,
romance, understanding, compromise and
tolerance. The depth of my love for you is
immeasurable. . . I would do anything for
you, because you deserve everything. . . .

Missing You

We all want to believe that
absence does make the heart
grow fonder.

I Miss You So Very Much

I miss you in my dreams, and I miss you in
my waking hours. Each time I close my eyes,
my vision of you is magnified. I feel your
presence everywhere as your scent hovers
in the air.

The taste of your lips linger forever on mine.
Yet, I long for more time after time. My body
aches for the touch of your caress from the
tips of my toes to the top of my head.

I miss you so very much, baby.
I wish that you were here with me. But, I'll
keep you close to my heart, that way we'll
never be apart, because I miss you so very
much, baby.

Missing You Deeply!

Each day that passes leaves me feeling lonelier than the day before. Although I know that you are away temporarily, I find myself missing you deeply!

At any given moment in time from sunrise at dawn till sunset at dusk as the moon revolves around the earth, I think of you as your image cloud my thoughts.

So, until we see each other again, memories of the color of your eyes, the touch of your lips, the scent of your being and the sound of your voice whispering in my ear will sustain me.

I Miss You. . .

I miss you on the days that we are not together, and I miss you the moment you hang up the phone. I want to be with you every second and have thoughts of you all day long.

I miss looking into your eyes as they stare deeply into mine. I miss being close to you and feeling the warmth of your body.

When I'm with you, time stands still . . . and all I could think about is keeping you near, because whenever we're apart, all I do is miss you.

I'm So Lost Without You

*The sun doesn't seem as bright anymore,
the nights seem a little darker, and I
miss the closeness we shared as we
cuddled in each other's arms. But, your
scent is on my pillows and somehow I
manage to sleep.*

*I don't know what to do with myself
when you're not around. Of course, I
have more time to think about life in
general, but most of the time, I'm
thinking of you.*

*I'm thinking of our passionate kisses, of
caressing you tenderly, evenings shared
in blissful silence and times of heated
discussions. I miss not having you here,
because I'm so lost without you.*

I Long to Feel Your Body
Close to Mine

*I long to feel your body close to mine.
I long to see that lovely smile on your face. I
have your picture by the side of my bed, but
it's not enough to take your place.*

*I always miss you when you're not around.
But what I miss most is not being able to
touch you when I need to feel close.*

*So, when I see you again, I'm going
to take you into my arms, caress the
length of your body and kiss you tenderly
until we both burn with desire.*

Longing for Your Caress

I don't know how much longer I can go on without the feeling of your touch upon my skin. I need you ever so close to me, and I am so hot for your love that I feel the heat rising within me and fear that my insides may burn from the intensity.

I find it difficult to focus on other things that require my concentration, because thinking of you has my mind in a fog. How much longer will it be before I can enjoy the pleasure of your tender caress upon my hungry body.

Evenings are the worst part of my day. Laying alone in bed without you can be so lonely, but then the memories of your touch come alive and often leaves me gasping in my sleep. But still . . . I am longing for your caress. . . .

Until Our Lips Meet Again

Until our lips meet again, every other thought drifting through my imagination is borne of you. Each thought is accompanied by visions of you that are tantalizing and teasing in the most seductive way.

Of course, I think of you intellectually as well, that is why I find you so captivating and difficult to forget when we are not side by side. Every moment we are distanced from one another, I find myself lost in time. The length of time is not a matter of concern, it is the deprivation I feel in your absence.

I do miss you even when we are apart for just a few hours. I miss the scent of you . . . the touch of you . . . the feel of you . . . and losing myself at just the sight of you. Being apart only leaves me wanting you more . . . until our lips meet again. . . .

Proposal

If you have been lucky enough to
have found someone who makes your
heart beat faster, who constantly takes
control of your thoughts, who respects you
and your opinion, who loves you just the
way you are, etc. Then, that may be the
person to whom you'll want to share your
life with in every way. . . .

To The Future

I look forward to the future with you in my life, standing by my side, believing in my dreams and sharing in my pain.

You satisfy me intellectually and physically, that's why I'm so in love with you. I want to spend the rest of my life showing you just how much!

So, if you promise to be my lover, my friend, and my confidante to all ends, then I promise to keep us both laughing, happy, and in love.

Without you, my life would be incomplete.

I Promise....

It's your face I want to see every morning when I arise, because you're everything I'll ever need or want in this lifetime.

I can't promise you a perfect world or a perfect life, but I promise to love you unconditionally and I'm willing to compromise.

I just want to make you happy, be supportive of your dreams and desires and hold you in my arms for comfort every evening when we retire.

Will You Love Me Forever?

You are perfection. . . .
Your beauty is mine to behold
Your eyes are bewitching
Your smile lights up the night
Your laughter fills the air
Your lips are sweet as honey
Your touch fills me with desire
You intoxicate me with your wit
I want to be your everlasting love
I want to be the star in your life
I want to share everything with you
I want our lives to be as one, because
Your love is like none I've ever known
But, will you love me forever?

Will You Share the Rest of Your Life with Me?

Will you love me when I grow old?
Will you love me unconditionally?
Will you care for me when I am ill?
Will you share the rest of your life
with me?

I want to fulfill all of your needs.
I want to succumb to your wildest desires.
I want to be the one that you confide in.
I want to share your happiness, your
pain and your sorrow.

Our love is deep enough to last an eternity
and strong enough to deal with uncertainty.
The future is ours to behold, if you'll share
the rest of your life with me.

Will You be My Forever Love?

There is no one else in this world that I would
rather share my life with than you. You have
enhanced my life in ways I would never have
thought possible. When I am with you, I see
things from a different perspective. We
complement each other in our ideas
and thoughts.

I have found in you a love that is truly
everlasting and deeply spiritual. A love that
is unconditional, emotionally fulfilling,
physically satisfying and mentally
stimulating. How could I possibly ask for
more?

We love each other madly, and I will love you
forever. I cannot imagine living the rest
of my life without you. With you, I feel I have
discovered another dimension to my being and
a purpose for my existence. Will you be my
forever love?

You're the One I Want

*Of all the things I have ever wanted in life,
none could measure up to my desire of
wanting and loving you. You're the one, I
want to come home to . . . night after
night. . . .*

*You're the one, whose lips I want to caress.
You're the one whose ear I want to nibble . . .
whose body I want to ravage . . . and whose
eyes I want to behold. You're the one . . . I
want to come home to night after night.*

*I want to hold you in my arms when nothing
else will do. I want to give you strength when
weakness intrudes. I want your troubles to
be my own and for you . . . never to suffer
alone. You're the one . . . I want to come home
to night after night.*

Apology

Sometimes you do things that you are
sorry for and wished had never happened
and sometimes there are things that
you wish you had done.

You're Not Answering My Calls

*I call you day and night, and I'm getting
quite uptight. I don't know if you're at
home or if you just refuse to answer
the phone.*

*I don't want you to be upset with me.
I didn't mean to hurt your feelings or to
make you so angry.*

*What do I have to do to get you to talk
to me again. I'm sorry for making you
feel the way that you do, and I'll do
whatever I can to make amends.*

I'm Sorry I've been
Neglecting You

Baby, I realize that I have not been spending
a lot of time with you. I have just been so
busy, and I know that I should have at least
called.

I don't want you to think that I forgot about
you or that I'm spending time with someone
else, because you're the only one I want.

So, please don't be angry with me, nor do I
want you to break up with me. I would like it
if you would be patient until we do get
together again very soon.

Forgive me?

I Never Wanted to Hurt You

I know there is nothing I can say that
would wash away the hurt and pain
that you are feeling right now.

It's impossible to predict what will
happen in life, and I have no excuse
for what I have done, but I realized
I made a mistake.

All I can say is that I am truly sorry
for breaking your heart. I only hope
that time does heal all wounds and
that you can forgive me.

I Didn't Mean to Hurt
Your Feelings

I want to apologize for the other night. I don't know what came over me, but I overreacted. I regret saying the things that I said, because that is not how I really feel.

I didn't mean to hurt your feelings, and I hope that you forgive me and accept my apology. I was feeling insecure, but that is no excuse for my behavior.

I would like to move our relationship forward in a positive direction and work through any problems that we may have, because I believe that what we share together is special.

Do you accept my apology?

I'm Sorry I Cheated on You,
Please . . . Forgive Me!

*I can't begin to express how sorry I am for
what I have done and for the hurt I have
caused you. I made a mistake. I came to the
realization that I care for you very much, and
I want our relationship to work.*

*I know that you have lost your trust in me
and that I must begin to rebuild that trust. I
know it will take time to get over the hurt and
that you may not be able to forget, but I hope
that you can forgive.*

*I'm willing to do whatever it takes to make
our relationship work, if you're willing
to give me another chance. I just don't want
to lose you, please forgive me. . . .*

I'm Sorry for Not Spending
Time with You

I hope there is no doubt in your mind how much I love you, miss you and want to spend time with you. However, I know I have been neglecting you, because I have been very busy at work. Even when I am home with you, we may not spend enough quality time together, if any at all.

I'm sorry I've been neglecting you. It's not something that I want to do, unfortunately, the circumstances are beyond my control at this time. It will not always be this way, and I will try my best in the future to spend as much time with you as I can. Please . . . do not be upset with me. I want to be with you as much as you want to be with me.

I know I have a lot of making up to do for not spending enough time with you. When the time is right, you will have my undivided attention and you can demand of me what you will as long as you don't take advantage. Again, I'm sorry for not spending time with you. I do love you very much.

I Will Make it Up
to You . . . My Love

My sweetheart, to whom I have
disappointed, please forgive me for
failing to do what I have
obligated myself to do.

Shame has befallen my soul, because I
have disappointed you so . . . but I will
make it up to you, if you will allow me
the privilege of doing so.

I hope that you are not too upset with
me. You know how deeply I care for
you, and I would not jeopardize what
I know to be your feelings towards me.
I will make it up to you . . . my love.

I'm Sorry for Not Being There
for You When You Needed Me Most

*Of all the times when you needed me most,
this was it, and I failed to be there for you.
Whatever excuse I have, it's not enough. It
may be impossible for me to make up for
something like this, but if I can do anything
at all for you at this late stage, I'll do it.*

*I hope you don't think any less of me,
although I can't blame you, if you do. I'm
a little ashamed of my behavior and want
desperately to atone for my non-responsiveness.*

*I don't want you to feel that you can't depend
on me anymore, because that would make me
feel more guilty than I already feel. I know
that I may have to gain your trust again as far
as reliability goes, and I 'm ready to do that.
So, please . . . don't exclude me from your life.*

I Didn't Want to Lie to You

I'm not sure what to say to you. Lying was not the answer. I only made things worse. I just didn't know what else to do. I guess telling the truth would have been the logical thing to do, but I didn't want to hurt you or wasn't sure how you would react. I just didn't know. . . .

Now that you do know, I hope we can work things out. I know my lying has damaged our relationship. I pray it's not damaged beyond repair. I know the "trust" issue has to be dealt with.

What do you want me to do? What will make things right between us or at least get us back on track to what we had before? What we had before may not have been perfect, but I really want to make things right. I am sorry for not being honest with you and for possibly totally destroying the trust you had in me. I didn't want to lie to you, and I know that was a mistake.

I'm Sorry for Standing You Up

I know you are probably a little upset with me or even disappointed with me and may not want to speak to me. I do understand your feelings completely. However, I want to apologize profusely for standing you up.

For reasons not worth detailing at this time, I was unable to notify you in advance to cancel. It probably doesn't excuse my not calling, but I hope you can forgive me.

If you do forgive me, I would like to make arrangements once again to get together with you. I do want to see you again, soon.

End of Relationship

Breaking up is sometimes hard to do and
sometimes it isn't. There are times, however,
when you need to be told how much you're
loved and needed and to be reassured of each
other's love and commitment. There are also
times when you realize that you let the love of
your life slip through your fingers. If you are
lucky, you may have a second chance to
win back the love of your life. However, there
are also times, when saying goodbye is best.

Baby. . . Please don't Leave Me!

*You're what I've been looking for in a
lover and in a friend, and yet I have been
unappreciative. I don't blame you for
wanting to leave me.*

*Perhaps I'm not used to being treated
so well, or maybe I'm afraid of
commitment. Whatever my reasons,
I realized that I don't want to lose you.*

*So, I'm begging you to give me another
chance. Let me back into your life.
I'll show you how much I really do care.*

Can we start over?

It's Time to Say Goodbye

I never wanted our relationship to end
like this, but I don't want to hurt
anymore. I have loved you and cried
for you, and now I am all cried out.

I dreamed of having a future with you,
of loving you forever, growing old
together, sharing good times and bad.
But dreams don't always come true.

Maybe we shouldn't concern ourselves
with why it didn't work, but begin to
start our lives anew, separately,
because it's time to say goodbye.

I Can't See You Anymore!

You catered to my every need and fulfilled my every wish. You made me laugh when I wanted to cry and you listened when I needed to be heard.

I needed to be loved more than I was being loved at home, and you were the one who loved me. But now, you're in love with me and demanding more of my time.

We knew from the beginning it could never be anything more than a love affair, because of obligations to others. I don't want to hurt you, but what else can I do. I can't see you anymore.

I Was a Fool to Walk
Out of Your Life

The day I walked out of your life was the biggest mistake I ever made. I never realized what I had. I thought I was leaving for something better.

As it turns out, leaving you has made me realize that you were the best thing I ever had. I know that I hurt you, and you'll never know how sorry I am.
I was a fool to walk out of your life.

But I want to know, do you still have feelings for me? Any feelings? Whether it's love or hate, is it too late for me to come back into your life? How can I win you over again?

I Want a Commitment from You

We are supposed to be in love, at least that's what we keep telling each other. We have invested time and emotions in this relationship, yet it is not moving in the direction that I would like it to go.

I want to believe that your feelings for me are real, because I have given you my heart and soul. We may not have a perfect relationship, however, I feel that it is worth continuing to nurture.

But, if you feel differently, I want you to tell me now! Otherwise, I want a commitment from you. I won't wait forever, and my life will go on with or without you.

I Want You Back in My Life

Ever since the day we parted, I find it difficult to laugh. Each morning when I awake, I feel a heaviness in my heart.

Whatever went wrong between us, it's not impossible to fix. I'm willing to try again, because real love needs nurturing.

When I think of you, I cry, not caring what people say. Your love is what I want and need. I want you back in my life.

I Just Want You in My Life

We've known each other for less than five years and in that time, you were always the best that you can be in anything. You were always supportive in everything that I chose to do. You're smart, ambitious and you would be a positive influence in anyone's life who is smart enough to recognize and appreciate that your friendship and love is priceless.

I was that lucky guy, but I wasn't smart enough to understand what goes into making a good and lasting relationship work due to my immaturity, recklessness and ignorance. I will always regret how much I hurt you. I never meant to hurt you.

Over the past 1½ years, I have grown tremendously, but I am still learning and will continue to learn and grow as a person. I want to be the best that I can be and the person I should have been when you were in my life. As much as I want you back in my life, I know that may not be possible right now, if at all. I would like to apologize for every thing I have done to hurt you, making you feel insecure and unhappy when we were together. I am willing to do whatever I need to gain you trust and heart again.

I Couldn't Love You... When I didn't Love Myself

As I think about my life and all that I have gone through, I am lucky to have met someone like you. You are what dreams are made of and although no one is perfect and no relationship is perfect, you were perfect for me. You did everything to make me happy, or so you thought. But my happiness wasn't your responsibility. Unfortunately, at the time, my unhappiness didn't allow me to appreciate what I had.

So, I wondered with all that I have, why am I not happy? Why is it difficult for me to love you? And why can I not accept your love and all that you want to share with me? I realized after spending time alone to collect my thoughts, analyze my feelings and explore my emotions that I didn't love myself. How can I accept and believe in your love when I can't even love and accept my own self. It was impossible to continue to be a part of your life. I needed to discover my own self and come to terms with who I am.

Throughout the process of my journey, I developed a love for myself. And, I want to apologize for any pain I may have caused you. I would like to be a part of your life again. I know what I ask is not that simple, but I wanted you to know how I feel. I want to know if it is possible to start over?

I Need Some Time Alone . . .
to Think Things Over

I want you to know that I care for you very much, but sometimes situations occur which forces us to acknowledge that things aren't always what they appear to be or what we want them to be.

I need to get my own thoughts together and decide in which direction my life is headed and in which direction I would like my life to go. There are issues that I need to solve for myself, so I need some time alone . . . to think things over.

Whatever decisions I make in the process of my soul searching, I cannot guarantee that the outcome will affect our relationship in a positive or negative way. I want to know if you will be there for me to share in my insights, and maybe together we can come to a mutual agreement regarding our future.

I Do Forgive You

It is not easy for me to forget that you have hurt me. Time has passed and the pain has eased. I never once let that pain interfere with my continuing to pursue my goals in life and to empower myself.

I realized that you have changed. You have matured and you realized what you have done was wrong and due to immaturity. I do forgive you, because I believe you are sincere in your apology.

Even though you hurt me, I've always thought about you. I always believed that when you finally matured and leave your past behavior behind, you would become the type of person I would like to be with, if our fate is to be together.

My Feelings for You Were Based on Lies

*You came into my life and captured my heart
by pretending to be something that you are not.
You have not been truthful and you have not
been honest about your intentions.*

*I have given my love to you freely, believing
that our feelings for each other are mutual.
And yet, I ignore that nagging ache deep
inside that tells me something is wrong,
because I want to believe that everything
between us is perfect.*

*I cannot go on any longer believing that your
love for me is as genuine as my love is for you.
It takes two people to build a strong and
meaningful relationship. However, if there
is no trust and honesty, then we have nothing
to build.*

You are Not Giving Our Relationship All That You've Got to Give

As much as I love you, I'm beginning to feel like this is a one-sided love affair. I find myself doing things to please you, but you are not trying hard enough to please me. You are not willing to compromise, nor do you take me seriously.

I am tired of having to make all the sacrifices, while you enjoy the fruits of my labor. If you cannot share equally in the responsibilities of our relationship, why do I need you? A loving and caring relationship between two people means sharing responsibilities, compromising and making sacrifices.

I want to grow old with you. I want to believe that we still have a future together, a future where I can count on you to be there for me when life is not so great, a future where there is trust, honesty and loyalty. I look forward to a future where we will complement each other in everything that we do and share. What do I have to do to get your attention?

I'm Tired of Feeling Used

I have always told you that whatever I have is yours, all you have to do is ask. You know that I am always here for you, whenever you need me.

I feel like you are taking advantage of my kindness, because you take and never give. I may have strong feelings for you, but it doesn't give you the right to take advantage of me.

I'm tired of being used, and I won't let you use me anymore. So, if you can't treat me the way that I should be treated, then I don't need or want you in my life. I deserve much better.

I have Never Cheated on You,
and I Never Will

I want you to know, I'm so in love with
you. You are the love of my life, and no
one else could ever take your place.

But, you've got to understand that if
I'm too busy to talk or too tired to spend
time with you, it 's not because I'm involved
with someone else, because I only have
eyes for you.

Every other thought I have is of you.
I don't want to lose you for something
that I didn't do. I need you to trust me
and to believe in my love.

It's Not You . . . It's Me

Whatever is wrong with our relationship, it has nothing to do with you. You have given me all the love that you can give. You have done everything that you can to make it work. I am the one with the problem.

I am not ready for all that you have to give me. I don't know if I ever will. Maybe it's time for us to go our separate ways, because you deserve better than what I have been able to give you. I can't give you what you want and need.

I want you to be happy and staying with me only makes you sad. If we can't make each other happy and fulfill each other's needs and desires, then maybe we shouldn't be together. Maybe we should both move on.

I'm Willing to Give Our Love Another Chance

No relationship is perfect, but what we had was good. We enjoyed each other very much. Yet, sometimes, no matter how good we think our relationship is or how much we think we are in love with each other, things happen that create tension or hurt in the relationship.

I was very hurt by what happened. I know that you have regrets. You tell me that you still love me. I am willing to give you the time that you need to sort out your problems and indecisions about your life, your feelings and about us.

I still love you very much, and I do want to share my life with you. I just want you to be sure about what you want, who you want and to be honest with yourself. If you want me in your life, I will be here for you, but I need to know that I am the only one that you want.

107

It's Time to Move On

I don't know how to say this without hurting your feelings, so I'll just say it. We've had good times and bad times, however, too much of one and not enough of the other and something missing in between.

I'm not blaming you for what went wrong or what didn't go right, because we're probably both to blame in one way or another. I am saying that I think it's time to end this relationship, because I am ready to move on with my life without you.

I'm sorry it didn't work out between us for whatever reasons and at this point and time, I am not interested in trying to make it work. I just want to part as friends and go our separate ways.

Please . . . Leave Me Alone!

I'm trying not to be nasty or mean to you.
I want to be civil about this, so I'll just
ask you nicely this time, please . . . leave
me alone !

I am not interested in getting involved
with you. I'm not even sure if I want to be
friends, because you are too demanding and
are constantly harassing me. I need my space!

I think you need to look inside yourself and
discover the reasons why you are acting this
way. When you are happy within yourself,
you'll find that you don't need to push yourself
on others.

Somebody Stole Your Heart Away!

I thought we were taking our relationship slowly not wanting to rush into anything too quickly, so I thought I had everything until you told me you were in love with someone else.

So, I wonder.... if you ever had any feelings for me. Was everything you told me a lie? I thought we had something special, something lasting, because we enjoyed being with each other, laughing and talking all the time.

But somebody stole your heart away, and I wanted to be the one. Even though you broke my heart, I'm willing to fight for your love, because I can't imagine not being able to hold you in my arms again.

Why did You Throw My Love Away?

Our bond as a couple was sealed . . . or so I thought. We shared times of joy, of sadness and of togetherness. We were so good together as a team, as lovers, as friends, as allies.

I didn't want it to be, but I felt you pulling away ever so subtly. I didn't want to acknowledge the faint ache in my heart. I'm still dumbfounded about the events of our relationship and what actually happened.

I know life has to go on . . . but I feel there's something missing. I feel I need an answer. I keep trying to figure out the exact point of no return. Tell me . . . why did you throw my love away?

Your Betrayal Hurt So Much!

My heart is broken. . . . I would never have believed that you could or world hurt me like this. I can't believe that you cheated on me! It feels like my heart has been wrenched out of my body, that's how much it hurt. I love you so much and now I'm left wondering how much do you really love me? I didn't realize we had problems and going outside of our relationship isn't going to help solve them.

Do I now have to wonder every time you kiss me or touch me . . . that you're thinking of someone else? Do I have to be suspicious when you glance in someone's direction when we're out together? You've broken my heart and our relationship. I can't even think straight right now . . . and I can't bear for you to touch me. I don't know if I want to stay with you or if I should.

I don't want to do anything rash in the heat of anger and hurt. I need to be calm, relaxed and clear headed before I make any decisions affecting my life with you. Is our relationship worth saving? Is this a deal breaker? Have you done it before? Will you do it again? I need to know why?

It's Time to go Our Own Separate Ways

Once . . . we might have had something good,
but that time has passed. We're both adults
with our own wants and needs in life.
However, our wants and needs are no longer
the same, if they ever were.

I need my own space. And, I don't need
anyone telling me what, where, how and when
to do anything. I run my own life. And, if
you're not enhancing it, then you're
disrupting it.

I want someone who's going to wipe the
teardrops streaming down my face. Someone
who knows when to take me into their arms to
console me or love me. Someone who can lift
me up and not bring me down. I want and need
someone who knows how to take control, but
who isn't controlling. So, it's time to go our
own separate ways, because you aren't that
someone, at least not any longer.

Fantasy of Love

Some fantasies are never explored,
but are better left to the imagination.
However, there are fantasies that can
and should be explored, fulfilled and
enjoyed by both.

The Seduction Fantasy

In anticipation of your arrival, I soak myself in a bubble bath scented with your favorite fragrance while sipping fine wine and forming mental images of what lay ahead...

With the music playing in the background, I am so wrapped up in my imagination that I fail to hear you come in. As you extend your arm to me, I step out of the disappearing bubble bath while following your gaze.

As you entice me with your eyes, you longingly look me up and down from head to toe. You then caress my soul with the touch of your fingertips as they glide seductively over my pulsating body.

The Pick-Up Fantasy

While sitting at the bar, I glance around at the other patrons and overhear snatches of conversations as I take a sip from my drink. I feel vulnerable and wonder if I should have come, but I decide to stay.

I glance toward the entrance as the door slowly opens and you walk in.... My body begins to tremble all over while my heart beat rapidly and weakness befalls me as I turn away quickly avoiding direct eye contact.

But, I cannot dismiss you so easily. I imagine tasting the sweetness of your lips as they hunger for mine and fall prey to your sensuality, when you suddenly appear before me to ask, if I am alone....

Riding the Waves

I awaken. . .to find myself in the middle of an island with no one else in sight, but I am not afraid. . . . I am surrounded by large tropical plants towering into the sky and as I too look upward, I am filled with a sense of calm passing through my body.

As the scent of fresh dew fill my nostrils, I hear the call of the ocean as the waves summon me to come forth. Piece by piece, my clothing falls away as I walk in a trance toward the open waters.

As I tread into the water, I am greeted by large waves that hover around me. I am suddenly lifted off my feet, falling backward as they pull back, then ferociously rush forward pushing me farther out. Floating on my back, they reappear, silently riding underneath me, caressing me gently.

Daydream

Still thinking about you as I step inside the room, I catch a glimpse of my reflection in the full length mirror as the damp towel wrapped loosely around my body falls carelessly to the floor. I pause a minute to admire my body, then close my eyes and imagine your arms wrapped tightly around me.

I can't release you from my thoughts, because I hear your voice whispering in the wind and feel a tingle in my toes as your lips wander aimlessly, kissing me gently and slowly while devouring the cherries and licking the whip cream from my body. . . .

Opening my eyes feeling somewhat exhilarated and dazed, I slowly adapt to reality. I glance one last time before retreating to the black chaise lounge where I lay down to listen to the wind through the open window.

After the Game

As the game ends, I turn off the TV set with
the remote and take the empty beer cans into
the kitchen. Immediately, my thoughts turn
to you, and I realize without really wanting
to admit that I do miss you and I long to be
with you.

With your image implanted in my mind,
I take a long cold shower. . . . Walking into
the bedroom after drying off, I turn on the
stereo to soft rock. I then lay down in the
nude reaching for the phone as I rock and
slide on top of soft satiny sheets.

Hearing my voice, you purr. . . like a kitten
sending chills tingling throughout my body
making my hairs stand on end. Your sultry
voice set my loins afire as you describe in
delicious detail the ways in which your
tongue will explore my flesh and
tantalize my senses.

Igniting Fires

Feeling extremely tired and fighting to keep my eyes open, I take a nice hot shower before calling it a night. Spraying myself with body satin spray from Coco Chanel, I massage it gently into my damp skin.

I slip on sexy red bikinis split in the middle with a matching sheer top and finally fall into bed laying on top of the covers feeling silky and sensuous all over. I immediately fall into a deep sleep as you sneak into my dreams....

Watching me silently, you crawl beside me, affectionately touching and kissing me from head to toe, inch by inch. I begin to feel a soothing warmth and only when the fire inside me ignites, do I realize, I am not dreaming....

Red Spiked Heels

Laying on the couch in the dark, my eyes closed,
I listen half-heartedly to the television when it
mysteriously shuts off and is replaced by soft, romantic
music filtering through the air. The only available light
coming from the moon, shining through the open
window creates silhouettes against the white walls.

Emerging from the shadowy doorway, slowly and
seductively in rhythm to the music wearing a long black
silk lounging robe, you advance towards me as if
gliding on air. Letting the robe fall from your shoulders,
you expose a sexy red satin corset trimmed in black lace,
red lace bikini panties, sheer black stockings held up by
a black garter belt and red spiked heels.

Moving your hips from side to side, your bosom
standing at attention has me mesmerized. Touching
your breasts with your fingertips, circling your nipples,
you move ever so close. As I glance at the shadow
dancing on the wall, you place your spiked heel between
my thighs, unsnapping the garter, sliding the stocking
seductively down your leg. I remove the spike and the
stocking and caress your leg, slowly moving upwards
until. . . .

Dripping in Honey

With the music drifting into the room, you walk in to find me shamelessly naked, eyes closed, sprawled lazily across the bed atop silky sheets sliding gently against my freshly scented skin. My arms lay loosely at my side, while my right leg is bent at the knee and my left leg hang slightly over the edge of the bed as your eyes move caressingly along the length of my body.

You disappear from the room returning with a bottle of honey. Slowly, kneeling over me, you brush your lips against mine. Seconds later, drops of honey circle my nipples one by one. I feel drops of honey dripping slowly down the center of my being, toward the universe of my womanhood. My desire is unmistakably awakened as I subtly move my hips as honey drip nonchalantly onto the sheets.

Just as the thought of wanting you reverberates throughout my body, your mouth gently devour my nipple, licking the honey slowly and deliberately like ice-cream. You follow the trail of honey with your tongue, licking and kissing with a hunger matched only by the craving you've created within me until you reach the peak of my existence at which point, I begin to writhe uncontrollably, gasping for breath.

I'm at Your Command . . .

*Minutes before your arrival, I prepare for the evenings'
rendezvous by placing soothing music on the CD player to
set the mood. Testing the temperature of the flowing bath
water, pouring capfuls of bath oil beads, a thick foam of
creamy white froth flourish. I arrange scented candles as
well as a bottle of champagne and a flute glass alongside
the edge. Upon your entrance, you greet me with suspicion
as the candle's sweet fragrance and smooth music capture
your attention. I proceed to escort you into a place of
forbidden pleasure. . . .*

*Without resistance, you allow me to remove your clothing
and as each piece is discarded, I become more aroused by
your nakedness. While you descend into the white froth, I
fill the flute for your sipping pleasure as you immerse
yourself and absorb the ambiance of the candle's aroma
and let your thoughts drift away with the soothing
melodies. . . .*

*With your eyes closed and your mind and body in a state
of suspension laying atop red satin sheets littered with
white rose petals, I slowly and deliberately drip coconut
oil along the length of your naked body. I massage the oil
into your skin inch by inch, taking special care to caress
those parts of your body so delicate and sensitive to my
gentle touch. Whatever more you desire, I am
at your command.*

Lickety Split

It's one o'clock in the morning on a cool wintry night, when I hear knocking at my door. As I open the door, a look of surprise cross my face, turning quickly into a smile. You step inside, staring at me hungrily. You follow me into the living room where I strike a match lighting the logs in the fireplace and suddenly flames jump wildly about creating a surreal atmosphere.

You unbutton your coat, letting it drop to the floor, taking me completely by surprise, your nipples staring me in the face as I turn to you. You begin to tingle inside, reaching for my hand guiding it between your legs to ease the throbbing. You bask in the pleasures as I skillfully work my fingers. At the same time, I cover your nipples with my mouth, licking and biting while you rub your fingers through my hair.

Before driving you completely over the edge, you disengage me, pulling me up, sliding your tongue into my mouth while I grab you from behind. You kiss me slowly moving from my mouth to my neck and chest, biting and sucking my nipples and slowly move down to my navel and on to the prize hanging between my legs. You lick me hungrily and eagerly before taking me into your. . . .

Reflection

Thoughts representing various
perspectives conveying ideas, issues
or situations derived from the
human experience.

I'm Only Human

I want to be loved and respected. And, I would prefer not to be judged based on my sex, race, religion, education, economic status, marital status, physical appearance or how I live my life. I just want to be understood and accepted for my differences.

I'm only human, so I will make mistakes in life. But, I will try to learn from them and not be deterred by failure or negative attitudes, because I have dreams I would like to fulfill, and I am willing to make sacrifices. I only ask that I not be kicked when I am feeling down, but that I am assisted in getting back on my feet.

Life is a Bitch! But, it is worth living . . . because in spite of the heartache and pain that I may encounter along the way, it won't last forever, and I can be sure that pleasure will eventually come my way. That's what life is all about! I have to take the good with the bad!

Why Can't I Find Love?

Am I not worthy?
Do I not bleed?
Do I not cry real tears?
Does my heart not ache?
I wish upon falling stars
I bask in the sunlight
The night deepens my mood
The rain hides my teardrops
I long to be loved and desired
And my body set on fire
I will love unconditionally
I am intellectual and emotional
I am sensitive and compassionate
So, why can't I find love?

The Magic of Love

When two people are in love
They're in a world excluding restrictions
The symptoms of love can be defined as infinite
You feel no hurt or pain
When she touches you
The electrical current loitering within you
Becomes possessed with a feeling
That cannot be denied
The invasion hits you like a tornado
And you enter into a bliss of shock
When you kiss her
Your lips are forever adhered
And to separate them
Would cause a massive disruption
In the atmospheric pressure
She is forever on your mind
Her beauty would stop the creation of man
Her voice seducing and angelic
And her whisper like a cloud of thunder
Reminiscing in the sky
To be in love is like living forever
When it dies, you die
Your mind wanders off
Your soul disintegrates
And your heart erupts

Wedding Vows

You have filled my life with an abundance of love, an overwhelming sense of security and voracious laughter. So I take you into the chambers of my heart, into the depth of my soul and into the circle of my life. . . .

When I am in your presence, I feel that I am the only one in your life who matters and that no one else exists. The time we have shared together is only but a minute moment of time compared to the eternity that we'll spend together, spiritually and emotionally for the rest of our lives.

My love for you grows deeper with each beat of my heart, and I will be there for you each and every day until the last breath that I take. I will listen to your hopes and dreams. I will do my best to satisfy your wants and desires. I will support you when you are feeling weak and stand by you in times of happiness as well as sorrow and through days of darkness.

You are the man in my life, and I want nothing more on this day, than for you to be my husband and I am honored to be your wife.

Our Love Is Eternal

*We begin a precious journey together, one in
which our lives will become linked emotionally,
spiritually, intellectually and physically under the
watchful eyes of God. Our love and faith in God
will give us strength to handle those things in life
that are difficult, painful and sorrowful as well
as cherish the moments that influence and
enhance our own existence.*

*We will seek the guidance of our almighty
God and travel to the ends of the earth to fulfill
our destiny, because our love is eternal and will
deepen with the passage of time as will the spirit
of our souls. . . .*

*The quality of life that we lead will be measured
by our commitment to each other and to ourselves
as we embrace our god given talents and accept the
essence of our own being while acknowledging our
limitations, yet striving to exceed those boundaries
put upon us by society and by our own selves.*

*With God in Our Lives Forever
Our Love is Eternal*

Life & Love

The meaning of life
Is it to love or to be loved?
Everyone wants to be loved
To be able to give love is special
To find true love is extraordinary
To love yourself is mandatory
To understand love is to experience love
When your life is filled with love
You'll never feel alone, and
If you believe in yourself
Then you believe in life, and
To have a purpose in life
Makes it more meaningful, but
Not necessarily easier to live
So, what makes life worth living?
Appreciating the good times, and not
Being overwhelmed by the bad times

What I Want From a Man

*I want a man who is secure in his manhood,
yet sensitive enough to express his emotions
without shame. I want a man who is strong in
his beliefs, yet flexible enough to accept change.
I want a man who has ambition and drive. I
want a man who will support me in my dreams
and goals.*

*I want a man who will pursue me relentlessly
but subtly. I want a man who will seduce me
intellectually and emotionally. I want a man
who is romantic and willing to explore new
frontiers and succumb to my wildest desires.*

*I want a man who is honest, trustworthy and
faithful. I want a man who will shower me
with love and affection. I want a man who
will comfort me when I'm feeling blue and
laugh with me at life's perplexities. But most
of all, I want a man who will treat me with
respect.*

*What I ask may be too much, but it is,
what I want from a man.*

Hung Over from Loving You

I used to cry myself to sleep at night after you walked out of my life. I thought I couldn't live without you, because of the emptiness I felt inside. But, I finally got myself together, and met another lover.

He's such a tender lover, but I feel there's something missing inside. I can't go on pretending anymore. It's not fair to me or my new lover thinking of you when I'm in his arms. I have to tell him that it's over.

I'm still hung over from loving you. It's your lips I taste when he kisses mine, and your face I see when I close my eyes. It's not fair to me or my new lover thinking of you, when I'm in his arms.

When Love Ends

I thought it was a love that would last forever
I wonder if it was really love at all
I imagined a future of love and commitment
Maybe I was the only one who was really in love
A love that is nurturing grows deeper
A love that is not grows cold, but
It hurts when you realize that it's over
I wondered if it was anything that I did wrong
But I know deep inside, I gave my heart and soul
And I'd rather be alone, than pretend all is well
I never thought I would have to start over
But I have so much to give to another lover
Someone who loves only me and no one else
Someone who thinks of me day and night
Someone who thinks of me as a bright star
Because when I give my love, I give it all
But a love that is true never grows old
So when I think of why it had to end
Maybe it was never really meant to be
But life goes on, and I'm happy to be free

In Loving Myself

In loving myself, I must be honest with myself in regards to who I am; what I am; my likes and dislikes; what I will and will not tolerate from myself and others; my limitations, accomplishments, ambition and the value I place on my life. I understand that life is what I make it and that my own happiness has to come from within. No one else is responsible for my life or my happiness.

It is no doubt at times overwhelming to think of all that I must encounter or have encountered throughout my life just to keep on living, if that is what I choose to do. No one has ever told me that living is easy and there are times when I may have made it much tougher than it ought to have been, because I don't always make the best decisions for myself or my body.

I know that deep within my soul is where I'll find myself. And, when I do find myself, I may even scare myself. But . . . I shouldn't retreat. I should continue to search until I am able to accept who and what I am. If I am not happy with all that I find, I am free to change, alter or develop any parts of my being, I feel is unacceptable. Because in loving myself, I must be honest with myself, if to no one else.

Memories Will Always Live On

When you lose someone who has been a special part of your life, you really only lose the physical part of their being. They will always be a part of your life in mind and spirit, because your memories will exceed the boundaries of time and the essence of who they were as a person will never fade.

You are privileged to have had this person in your life and to have been able to share experiences with each other. Those experiences are a lifetime of treasures that are priceless.

Life is precious, and if it has been fulfilling and satisfying, then it has been lived. Grief should turn into a celebration of life, yet take time to grieve if you must, but remember, you are loved and always will be from the heavens above.

Thank You for the Privilege of Taking Out Your Daughter

I can't imagine what it's like to have a daughter. I imagine you must have a very special relationship. It must also be difficult to realize that she's grown up to be an independent young lady with a mind of her own.

You must be very proud of her and what she has accomplished so far in her life. I know you want the best for your daughter and want her to be happy, safe and secure in whatever she chooses to do.

I would also like to say that I think your daughter is a very fine young lady, and I thank you for allowing me the privilege of taking her out and spending time with her.

Motherhood

The day a woman becomes a mother, her life changes forever. Her life is no longer her own, but must be devoted to raising her child for the next eighteen years or more.

In a world full of uncertainties, she must do her best to teach her child the difference between right and wrong, about love, hate, compassion, humanity, sharing, self-worth and to give her child the best education possible. Her job is not always easy and most of the time, she is learning as she goes, so she makes mistakes along the way.

Her goal is to teach her child about life and hope that he or she grows up to be a successful and productive adult in society.

Motherhood is an Honor . . .
Motherhood is for Life . . .

A Mother's Love . . .
                    is Like No Other

Your love is unconditional
Your love lasts forever
Your love is very special
Your love is like no other
You try not to be judgmental
You try not to be too critical
You try to be honest and open-minded
You try to be considerate and hospitable
You're not always appreciated, yet
Your time is often devoted to others
Your love can never truly be replaced
Your love is deep, forgiving and forever
You are one in a million
You should be cherished . . .
                    like a precious jewel

To My Son/Daughter
You'll Always Have My Love

Raising children is not an easy task. You learn as you go,
and you hope that you don't make too many mistakes.
But, you do make mistakes, because you are human.
I am not proud of the circumstances that led to the
period of time that we were not together, and I can't
begin to express the feelings I had when you came
back into my life.

Over the past several years, we've had the opportunity
to build our relationship and although it may have been
difficult at times, it was definitely worth it to have
you in my life again. We have grown closer and we
have so much more to look forward to in our lives
for the future. We won't always agree with one
another, but we can at least respect each other and
be accepting of the person each of us has become.

I want the communication between us to always
remain open. I want you to feel free to discuss anything
that is on your mind. If I cannot help you, I will do my
best to comfort you and to be understanding. Having you
in my life has made my family complete. You will always
have a special place in my heart. You will always have
my love. I do love you, and I want us to always be as
close as we are now.

Who Am I . . . Really?

Who am I . . . Really? I was born into this world a free spirit, but I need to find my way to discover my true purpose in life. Will I take medicine to the next level by incorporating eastern and western philosophies? Will I re-discover the natural resources of nutrient based soil that once grew whole foods? Or, will I become a champion for human rights for those less fortunate who cannot represent themselves? Who and what am I destined to become?

Wherever my destiny takes me, I have to acknowledge the world as it is up to this point. The good, the bad and the ugly. International terrorism. Domestic terrorism. Children being abused. Citizens being attacked in the streets. Politics gone to hell! Fake news. Fake food. Scammers. Identity theft. Not enough of this, too much of that!

In my search of self which is not independent of the search for my understanding of the human condition-- if I am to be a guiding light. I must be able to contemplate answers to questions that may be asked of me such as why can't I live my life the way I want? Why do I have to believe in what you believe? Shouldn't we be free independent thinkers that make the world go round?

Life is a Precious Gift

With only one life to live, living should be given
the highest level of learning, growth, aspirations,
social consciousness, enjoyment and appreciation.
But, the opportunities for such are not always
available or within reach. There are those who
may unfortunately, never realize life's potential.

I am responsible for my own life and my own
happiness. I'm responsible for making my life
meaningful and fulfilling. Even so, each goal that
I pursue will not always come to pass, even when I
believe that it should. When it does, then it was
meant to happen at that particular time. If it
doesn't, then I have to accept it and move on to
other endeavors. I have choices in life and the
choices I make, I have to live with. We all make
mistakes, but if I'm lucky, sometimes my mistakes
can be corrected and a lesson learned.

However, living also requires strength to deal with
life's uncertainties. Sometimes a life is cut short,
and I may find it difficult to understand why and
blame others and may have my beliefs shattered. It

could be that every life has a purpose, although I may not know what it is. Sometimes, I am taught lessons, I do not realize I am learning. Life is not perfect. So, there will be times of disappointment, sorrow, loss and devastation that might at the time seem to dismantle the center of my inner world. But . . . life does go on and in time, I learn to adjust.

With all that living entails . . . the good, the bad, and the ugly . . . life is still a precious gift. I can choose to be whatever I want to be. When I fail at something, all is not always lost. I can try and try again or choose to try something new. I am only as limited as my imagination, my dreams, my drive and my ambition. The beauty of life is what I make it.

Life is complicated, but . . . that's the reality of living.

About the Author

Rhonda always wanted to write greeting cards and remembers writing her own verses inside greeting cards she bought as a child. Later, wanting to be a hit songwriter, she called Local 802 and spoke to Lenny Calderone. He helped her find someone who would agree to write music to her six poems. After several calls, Lou Toby, a musical director agreed to a consultation. They met and he tore her work apart telling her that a song is like a composition. It has a beginning, a middle and an end. If she wasn't serious, she would never have gone back the following week with re-writes. They met once a week for four hours for two months and continued via snail mail for two years. He taught her how songs are structured which was invaluable to her writing love letters years later.

Rhonda lives in NYC and has an MS Degree in Social Research from Hunter College. She has an online knitwear store which is continually developing at www.deloneaknits.com. Other passions are photography and acting.

www.ingramcontent.com/pod-product-compliance
Lightning Source LLC
LaVergne TN
LVHW011331080426
835513LV00006B/290

www.ingramcontent.com/pod-product-compliance
Lightning Source LLC
LaVergne TN
LVHW011337080426
835513LV00006B/396